HOW TO TELL TIME

POEMS

TERRY McCARTY

For Felix and Kabuki

and, especially, Valarie

Table of Contents

FIRES OF YOUTH

left the house

climbed into the car

went with my parents

to places where something just ignited:

the furniture store downtown

an abandoned church on Highway 25

and all I could see was

bright yellow-orange color

smoke pouring out of windows

firemen arriving just in time

>

too young to understand concepts

like impermanence, destruction

and how lives could change--or end

>

staying quiet

in a 65 Malibu

at a safe distance

wondering how high

the fire would climb

before touching the night sky

HEAR THE POP (1970)

Hear the pop

Then the cop

Yells STOP!

That's the end

Of the payday

As the box

Of Dope sits

On the ground

As your hands

Raise up high

Above your head

Then behind back

As handcuffs click

You're shoved into

Cruiser back seat

Cop smiles as

Siren turned on

And you think

Will I have

To cut hair

For Judge's sake

Will my lawyer

Say I'm a

Good Boy

From a Good

Family who never

Got into this

Kind of trouble before

And I'm in

My sophomore year

Of college

Hoping not to

Be drafted

All of this

Because I listened

To a friend

Of a friend

Have mercy Judge

HELLO TIMES PAST

walk happy through shopping mall

new vinyl/nylon marching band jacket

maybe she'll notice and compliment

oh no, she's not at department store job

too early to go home

no movies starting soon

walk to Disc Records

flip through albums and 8-track tapes

three male classmates come up and say

they're tired of me because

my grades are too good

and their parents hold me up

as some kind of role model

one of them slaps me

in the back of the head

before telling me I need to fail

at least one exam

to take the heat off of them

then he calls me "damn queer"

before they strut away

it's only junior year

and this hell rarely stops being fresh

POOR LISTENER

too much time alone

too few encounters with others

outside the spheres of school and work

fifteen-year-old boy calls girl on phone

can't understand why she says no

twenty-eight-year-old man calls woman on phone

can't understand why she changed her mind

even when she tells him about the man who hurt her,

he goes ahead and asks once again

saying I'm not like that

and then, poor listener that he is,

gets hurt and tearful when the woman

abruptly hangs up the phone

in the midst of his special pleading

leaving him only a dial tone to speak to

man heading south of age fifty-five

reads the news stories

about males who keep coercing,

continue pressuring, applying force

he finally listens

MEASURING UP

where you are

versus

where you should be

the hammer pounding nails

into my conscious mind

the recycled straw stirring the glass

of stomach medicine

on late sleepless nights

>

trying so very very hard

to at least meet expectations

roll that boulder uphill FAST

silent prayer for it to stay in place

cringing when it dislodges

smashes into carefully built fence

supervisor strides towards me

like a Western trail boss

in the middle of a cattle drive

promise I'll do it better next time

glad he didn't say THAT f-word

go straight home

double over in pain

almost an hour in bathroom

>

want tomorrow to be better

keep breathing in and out for calm

can't help but continue thinking about

where I am

versus

where I should be

GOOD SOLDIER

open both eyes

look at hallway's end

start walking

follow most rules

forget some of them

bruised knuckles

deep red voices

vibrating eardrums

notes in your permanent file

warnings you'll be fired

if you fail to park

in the proper place

rarely get compliments

unless it's evaluation time

decide if the door

at the end of the hallway

is worth opening

after years of repetitive motions

and one step forward

for every two debits back

once you're promoted,

don't be that person

who hollers/punches/kneecaps

instead, you can be the mentor

only a few people

took the time to be with you

when it's time for newcomers

to take the employee walk

wherever it may lead

AFTER BEING TOLD NOT TO WORK

there are things to miss

about the old job:

the friends glad to see you

most of them empathizing

and agreeing with every vent

about changes in policy

and how things used to be more efficient

but you don't miss the colleagues

who were only nice to you

until promotion

and then they didn't have to care

or even speak to you anymore

clean out the desk

all the cubicle items stored

in spare room at home

learn how to cope with no deadlines

entire days where you feel like

you're getting used to

at least one phantom limb

NO CHILDREN

a child past childhood

my own parent in adulthood

sometimes responsible

often too permissive

married later than others

thought I was too old to be Dad

still lapsed into unchecked emotions

not finding the proper balance

between achievement and disappointment

we visit our niece in the Midwest

only viewing snippets of growth:

baby, toddler, preschool

look at pictures of friends' children

and grandchildren on social media

click "like" or add a heart emoji

wish them well

as if they were our own

ate a wonderful chopped vegetable salad
with ten-dollar grilled salmon on top
at a new restaurant
inhabiting an old building
at the corner of 4th and Main Street
after dessert, on the way to the men's room,
viewed pictures of the landmarks
of an earlier Los Angeles
(Bunker Hill, the original Pershing Square)
altered or deleted by Progress
then drove to Disney Hall
got lost trying to find REDCAT,
noticed young people
wanting to be famous actors or models
using the upstairs ampitheater for a photo shoot--
and I wondered if the great Frank Gehry
would mind his grand silver creation
used as a backdrop for headshots

WORD RETRIEVAL

It's....

Word appears in mind's eye

But mental eyeglasses of at least +5.00

Are needed to determine what it is

It's....

Wait a few minutes

Perhaps an hour

Maybe the word appears on its own

It's...

The word doesn't arrive

Turn to spouse and begin

A description/definition/pantomime

It's....

Spouse says the word

You're relieved,

Thinking it's because

You haven't said this word

Within the past few weeks

Resolve to remember it

From now on

Hope this is only normal aging

And nothing worse

GOODBYE TO SOME OF IT

spent lots of nights out but still returned home

in time for the wife-to-be to arrive from work

all those younger people who would hear words

while sitting at tables writing words of their own

never could do two things at once in public

I'd listen then go home and write in the living room

almost everyone could mine for riches

before only one variety of gold became the standard

the pans and axes began to cost too much

small ambition, smaller gift of gab

too much opinionating against the tide

leave when you know you won't be missed

out but not down

mindburned but still functioning

assembling words to read aloud someday

even if it's only for an audience

of quizzical cats

wondering what daddy's really saying

YOUR FRANK BUTLER

I'll be Frank Butler

to your Annie Oakley

providing velvet gloves

so you don't have to handle

lead bullets and shotgun shells

>

I'll be your shoulder pillow

for rough train rides

on long cold nights

through endless prairie

>

I've fired my pistols

smashed most targets

bowed to standing ovations

now it's time to step away

>

you're better than I ever was

please keep doing

what foolish people say

women should never do

FEBRUARY 9, 1988

I went forward

Into a slightly charted land

Planting my flag in a suburb

Occasionally wrapped in smog

Drove to Culver City Target

For a cheap answering machine

Almost got lost in Venice

But I knew I'd find my way eventually

Swore to the City of Glendale

That I wasn't a Communist

Got a three-day-a-week library job

Performed shelving and microfilm threading

Co-workers held a body-length mirror

For me to view every inch

Of my social maladjustment

And that's how my life in California began

Drifted into movie and TV extra/stand-in work

Found time to volunteer at American Film Institute

Made a few genuine friends

Later traded the entertainment factory

For True Love that came and never left

Plus the attraction of writing poems

And the anticipation of learning more

Of course, there were missed opportunities and regrets

But I believe I'm better off

For embracing risk

Instead of staying in Texas and New Mexico

Preparing for Civil Service

To throw me a safe lifeline

OTHER BOOKS BY TERRY McCARTY:

HOLLYWOOD POETRY: 2001-2013

INTERLOPER

WICHITA FALLS: 10TH ANNIVERSARY EDITION

FROM OBSCURITY WITH LOVE: POEMS 1997-2017

POEMS BELOW THE LINE: B-SIDES

NEVER MET BUKOWSKI

IMPERFECTIONIST

REWRITES

ONE CORNER OF THE SKY

ANTHOLOGIZED IN THE FOLLOWING BOOKS/PUBLICATIONS

POETIC DIVERSITY (online e-zine edited by Marie Lecrivain)

A POET IS A POET NO MATTER HOW TALL series

(edited by Raundi Kai Moore-Kondo)

THE LONG WAY HOME: THE BEST OF THE LITTLE RED

BOOKS SERIES (edited by R.D. Raindog Armstrong)

SO LUMINOUS THE WILDFLOWERS (Tebot Bach Press)

SNORTED THE MOON & DOUSED THE SUN

(edited by Deanne Meeks Brown and Raundi Moore-Kondo)

1001 NIGHTS: TWENTY YEARS OF REDONDO POETS AT

COFFEE CARTEL 1998-2017

(edited by Jim Doane and Larry Colker)

VAN GOGH'S EAR (edited by Tina Ayres)